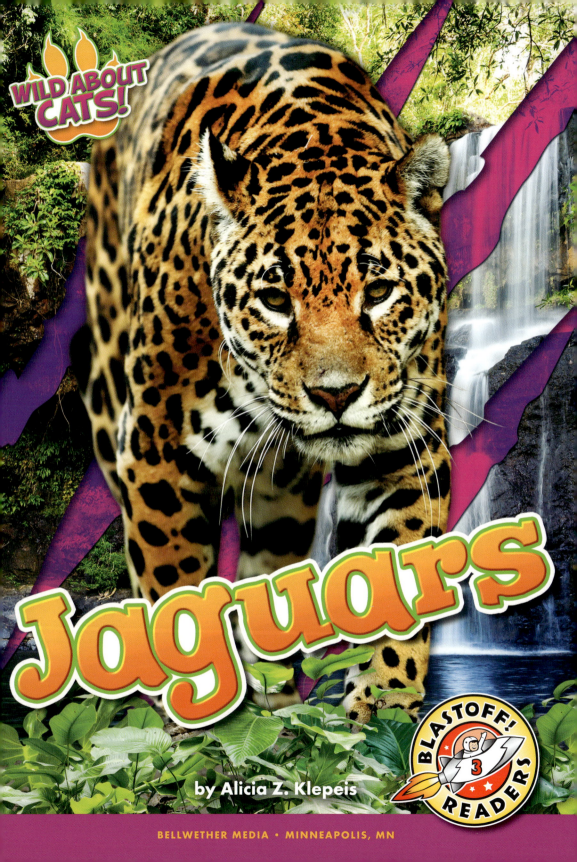

Blastoff! Readers are carefully developed by literacy experts to build reading stamina and move students toward fluency by combining standards-based content with developmentally appropriate text.

 Level 1 provides the most support through repetition of high-frequency words, light text, predictable sentence patterns, and strong visual support.

 Level 2 offers early readers a bit more challenge through varied sentences, increased text load, and text-supportive special features.

 Level 3 advances early-fluent readers toward fluency through increased text load, less reliance on photos, advancing concepts, longer sentences, and more complex special features.

★ **Blastoff! Universe**

Reading Level

 Grade K 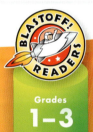 Grades 1–3  Grade 4

This edition first published in 2024 by Bellwether Media, Inc.

No part of this publication may be reproduced in whole or in part without written permission of the publisher. For information regarding permission, write to Bellwether Media, Inc., Attention: Permissions Department, 6012 Blue Circle Drive, Minnetonka, MN 55343.

Library of Congress Cataloging-in-Publication Data

LC record for Jaguars available at: https://lccn.loc.gov/2023046578

Text copyright © 2024 by Bellwether Media, Inc. BLASTOFF! READERS and associated logos are trademarks and/or registered trademarks of Bellwether Media, Inc.

Editor: Betsy Rathburn   Designer: Brittany McIntosh

Printed in the United States of America, North Mankato, MN.

Table of Contents

What Are Jaguars?	4
So Many Spots	8
Super Senses	12
Growing Up	18
Glossary	22
To Learn More	23
Index	24

What Are Jaguars?

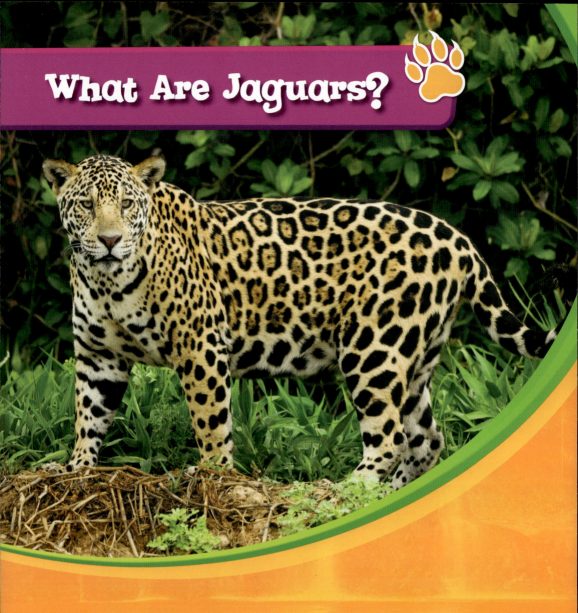

Jaguars are big cats that like water. They are strong swimmers. They hunt both on land and in water.

They live in many **habitats**. They often prowl **wetlands**, grasslands, and **rain forests**.

Jaguars are found in the Americas. Many live in the Amazon Rain Forest and the **Pantanal**.

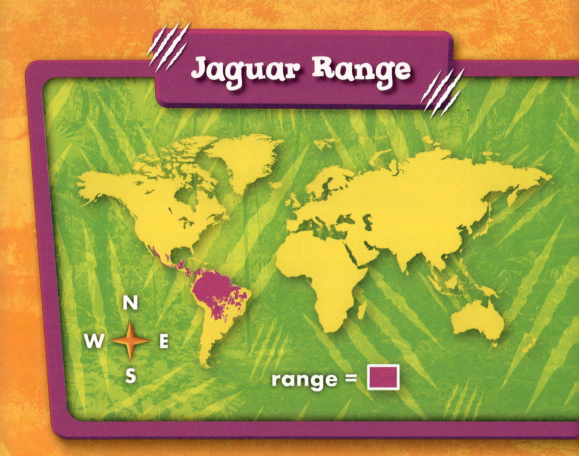

Jaguars are **near threatened**. Their numbers are dropping. This is because of hunting and habitat loss.

So Many Spots

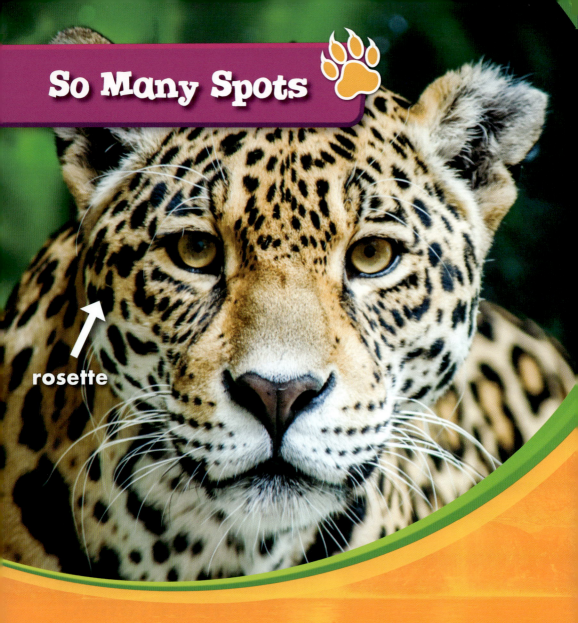

rosette

Most jaguars have yellow or tan fur. Their coats are covered with spots called **rosettes**.

Jaguars have **retractable** claws and powerful jaws. These help them catch and take down **prey**.

Identify a Jaguar

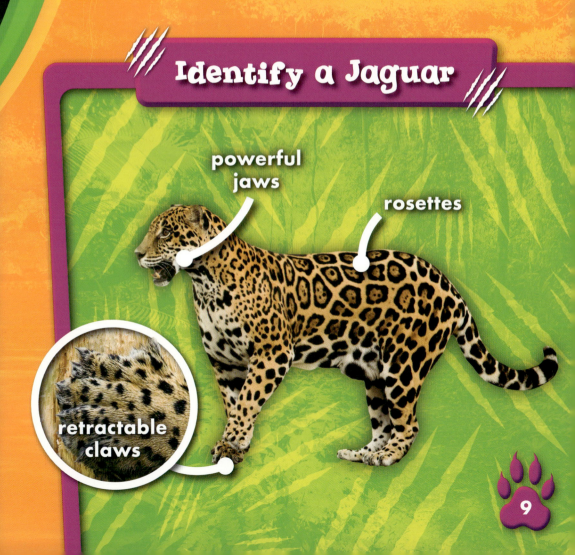

powerful jaws

rosettes

retractable claws

Adult jaguars can reach more than 6 feet (1.8 meters) long. Their tails add up to 3 feet (0.9 meters) to their length!

Size Comparison

house cat

height at shoulder
around 10 inches
(25 centimeters)

length (without tail)
around 18 inches
(46 centimeters)

jaguar

height at shoulder
over 24 inches
(61 centimeters)

length (without tail)
over 72 inches
(183 centimeters)

Jaguars can weigh over 300 pounds (136 kilograms).

Super Senses

Jaguars have excellent senses. Their strong hearing and sense of smell make them great hunters.

They often sneak up on prey. Then, they **pounce** and bite! They may also draw in fish by dipping their tails into water.

Jaguars are **carnivores**. They eat many kinds of animals. Capybaras are a favorite food.

Jaguars also eat tapirs, deer, and birds. They hunt fish, turtles, and caimans.

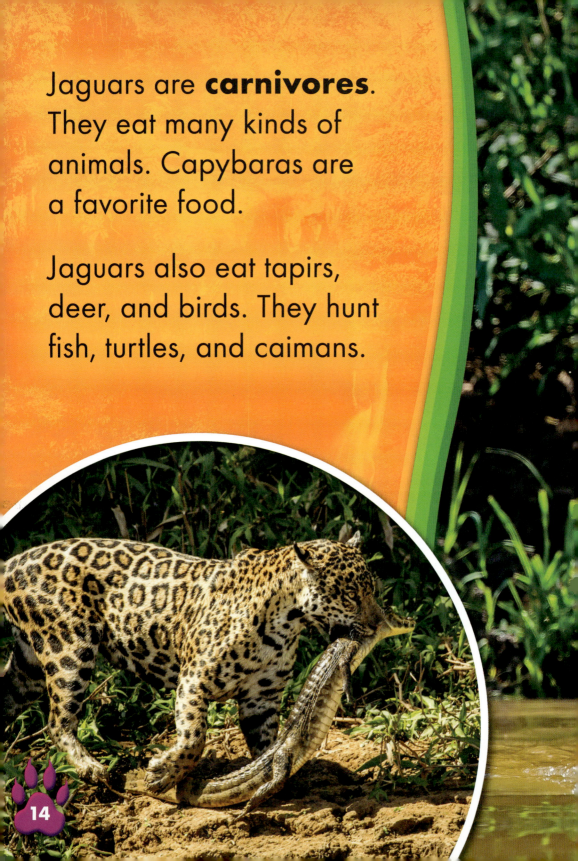

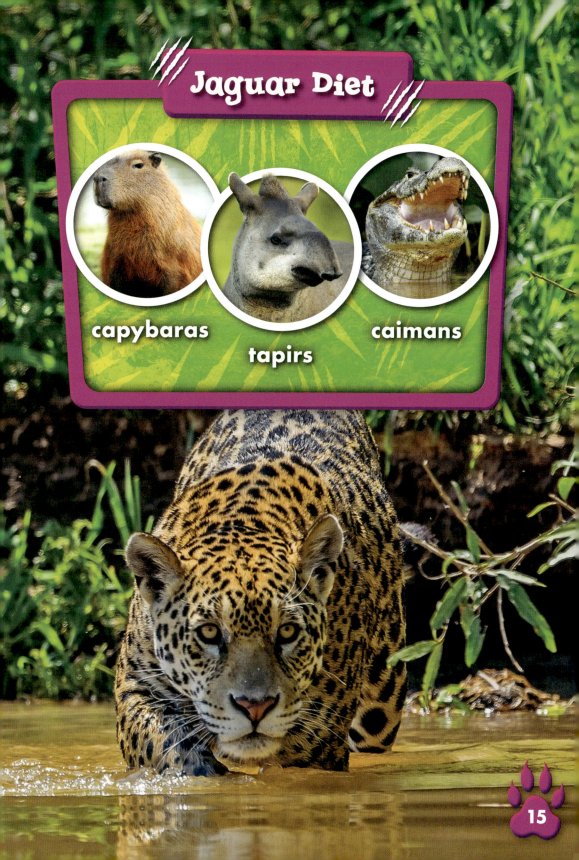

Jaguar Diet

capybaras
tapirs
caimans

Jaguars are mostly **solitary**. They need big home ranges to survive.

They mark their **territory** with pee and poop. They also leave claw marks on trees. Other jaguars stay away!

Growing Up

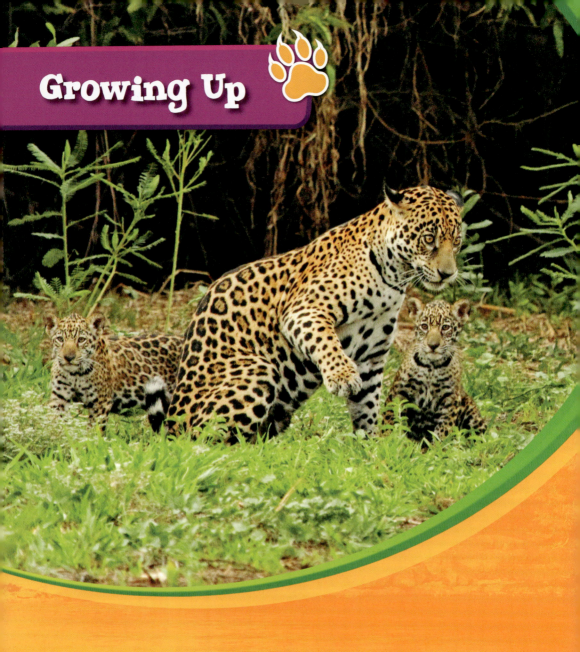

Female jaguars often have babies in the rainy season. They find food more easily at this time.

They usually have two cubs. Cubs like to play. They chase and practice fighting.

Baby Jaguars

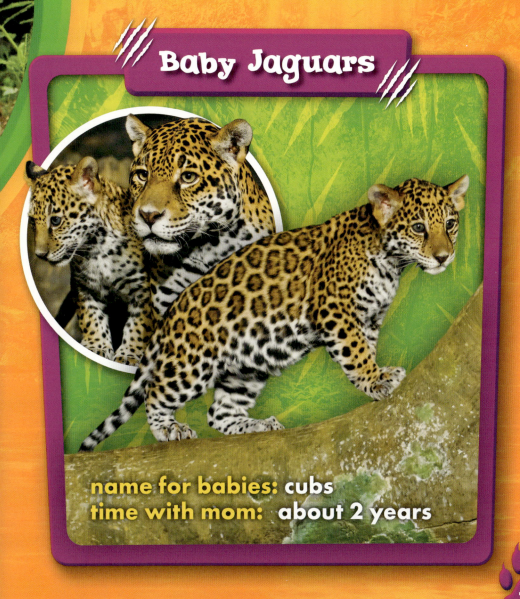

name for babies: cubs
time with mom: about 2 years

Cubs learn to hunt from their mom. They learn how to find and take down prey.

After about two years, cubs are grown up. They are ready to explore on their own!

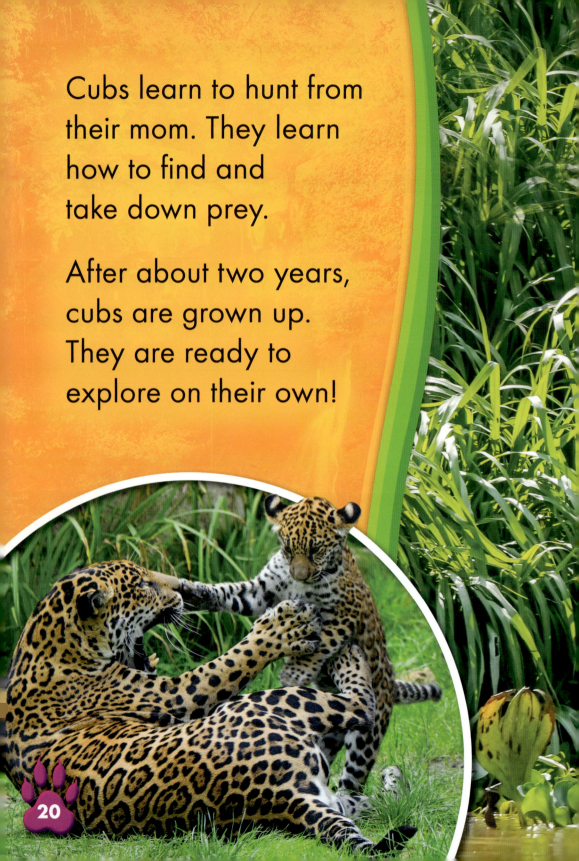

Glossary

carnivores—animals that only eat meat

habitats—land areas with certain types of plants, animals, and weather

near threatened—having a small or shrinking population and at risk of dying out

Pantanal—a huge wetland that covers parts of Brazil, Bolivia, and Paraguay

pounce—to suddenly jump onto something

prey—animals that are hunted by other animals for food

rain forests—thick, green forests that receive a lot of rain

retractable—able to be pulled back in

rosettes—dark spots on a jaguar's fur

solitary—living alone

territory—the land area where an animal lives

wetlands—areas of land that are covered with low levels of water for most of the year

To Learn More

AT THE LIBRARY
Bodden, Valerie. *Jaguars*. Mankato, Minn.: The Creative Company, 2023.

Klepeis, Alicia Z. *Leopards*. Minneapolis, Minn.: Bellwether Media, 2024.

Mills, Andrea. *Big Cats*. New York, N.Y.: DK Publishing, 2019.

ON THE WEB

FACTSURFER

Factsurfer.com gives you a safe, fun way to find more information.

1. Go to www.factsurfer.com.

2. Enter "jaguars" into the search box and click 🔍.

3. Select your book cover to see a list of related content.

Index

Amazon Rain Forest, 6
bite, 13
carnivores, 14
claws, 9, 17
color, 8
cubs, 18, 19, 20
females, 18, 20
food, 13, 14, 15, 18
fur, 8
grasslands, 5
habitats, 5, 7
home ranges, 16
hunt, 4, 7, 12, 14, 20
identify, 9
in the wild, 21
jaws, 9
near threatened, 7
numbers, 7
Pantanal, 6
play, 19
pounce, 13
prey, 9, 13, 14, 15, 20
rain forests, 5, 6

rainy season, 18
range, 6, 7
rosettes, 8
senses, 12
size, 10, 11
size comparison, 11
sneak, 13
solitary, 16
tails, 10, 13
territory, 17
water, 4, 13
wetlands, 5

The images in this book are reproduced through the courtesy of: Mikadun, front cover (jaguar), p. 16; Cocos.Bounty, front cover (background); Anan Kaewkhammul, pp. 3, 9 (jaguar); Octavio Campos Salles/ Alamy, p. 4; Westend61 GmbH/ Alamy, p. 5; milosk50, p. 6; zemkooo, p. 8; SteveAllenPhoto, pp. 9 (inset), 17; Gerald Corsi, pp. 10-11, 14-15; Nynke van Holten, p. 11 (house cat); Martin Mecnarowski, p. 11 (jaguar); Jo Reason, p. 12; Gurkan Ozturk, p. 13; Danita Delimont/ Alamy, p. 14; Wirestock Creators, p. 15 (capybara); Erni, p. 15 (tapir); blickwinkel/ Alamy, p. 18; Kris Wiktor, p. 19 (inset, cub); Nature Picture Library/ Alamy, p. 20; Uwe Bergwitz, pp. 20-21; Ana Vasileva, p. 23.